## Praise for Fox Doesn't Wear A Watch

At once enlightening, inspirational, and pleasantly whimsical, Jacob's skilled writing and grounded inquisitiveness shine as both an accomplished educator and a committed and humble learner. *Fox Doesn't Wear a Watch* leads readers through very personal stories and reflections yet is highly relatable through its themes that seek to reach all of humanity. Although Jacob doesn't shy away from critiques of colonialism and its manifestation in present-day Indigenous struggles, the overarching message gently invites all readers to reflect and learn from the lessons posed by the ultimate teacher—the land itself.

—Dr. Clint Carroll (Cherokee Nation), author of *Roots of Our Renewal: Ethnobotany and Cherokee Environmental Governance*

Michelle M. Jacob has given us another beautiful book. The narrator of this collection provides a warm, wise presence, and the stories offer hope, humor, guidance, and medicine for readers of all ages. These stories—and their lessons—are wonderful and essential companions.

—Beth Piatote (Nez Perce), author of *The Beadworkers: Stories*

*Fox Doesn't Wear a Watch* is masterful storytelling. Michelle M. Jacob writes to connect, reaffirm, and teach. This collection of stories will inspire readers to slow down and take time to appreciate their world in a whole new way.

—Lori Tapahonso (Diné / Acoma Pueblo), Lane Community College

*Fox Doesn't Wear a Watch* is a special and sacred book. The writing is beautiful, insightful, and timely.

—CC Wright (Klamath Tribes), Tribal Policy Analyst

The stories in *Fox Doesn't Wear a Watch* are understandable, relatable, and inviting.

—Brook Colley (Wasco / Eastern Cherokee, Enrolled Eastern Band of Cherokee Indians), associate professor of Native American Studies at Southern Oregon University

## Also by Michelle M. Jacob

*Yakama Rising: Indigenous Cultural Revitalization, Activism, and Healing*

*Indian Pilgrims: Indigenous Journeys of Activism and Healing with Saint Kateri Tekakwitha*

*On Indian Ground: A Return to Indigenous Knowledge: Generating Hope, Leadership, and Sovereignty through Education in the Northwest* (co-edited with Stephany RunningHawk Johnson)

*The Auntie Way: Stories Celebrating Kindness, Fierceness, and Creativity*

*Huckleberries & Coyotes: Lessons from Our More than Human Relations*

# Fox Doesn't Wear a Watch
## Lessons from Mother Nature's Classroom

Written by
Michelle M. Jacob

Illustrated by
Crystal L. Buck

## ANAHUY MENTORING, LLC
EXCELLENCE IN INDIGENOUS METHODS

Author royalties are donated to the Sapsik'ʷałá Program at the University of Oregon to support the next generation of Indigenous teachers. By purchasing this book, you are supporting Indigenous self-determination in education. Kw'alanúushamash! (I am grateful to you!)

ISBN (paperback): 978-1-7346151-4-2

ISBN (e-book): 978-1-7346151-5-9

Cover design by Christopher J. Andersen

Cover illustration by Crystal L. Buck

https://anahuymentoring.com
https://auntieway.com

This book is dedicated to all my Academic Aunties who, in my many years as a student, guided me, supported me, and—through their kind words and high expectations—asked me to reach my highest potential. How lucky I am that they continue to do so. Aunties are awesome!

# Contents

# Introduction: Continually Filling Our Baskets

I love witnessing seasonal changes. Mother Nature is quite the teacher, the entertainer, when she shows us these beautiful real-life dramas. As I write this, it's late spring in the northeastern edge of Nch'i Wána's (Columbia River) watershed. The freshwater lakes in the Flathead Valley are gorgeous, and the sacred water will flow from the homelands of Salish/ Sqelixʷ, Kootenai/ Ktunaxa, and Pend d'Oreille/ Qíispé peoples downstream to my Yakama Indigenous homeland and into our sacred river, Nch'i Wána, and then beyond to Atáchiish (Pacific Ocean). Water connects so many diverse peoples and reminds us that our futures are always intertwined.

On this fine morning, I am treated to a tug-of-war between chilly rain and warm sunshine. The back-and-forth makes me appreciate the particular beauty each weather shares. Today, in the brisk wind, Niní (Aspen tree) leaves dance and sing their chorus. Like all choruses, they are sharing a message; however, I can't quite tell what their words are.

Because it is cloudy and cold today, it feels like a good day to sit and ponder.

Something I've been pondering lately are the larger lessons we can learn from observing seasonal changes. I wonder, too, what we can learn from other cycles in our life: the ups and downs and routines.

If you're like me, you enjoy the anticipation of flipping the calendar page to the next month, those tidy squares providing a sense of order, waiting to be scheduled, a skill I learned in over two decades as a student in Western education. I eagerly look forward to seeing what pretty picture will adorn my next calendar page. This month I see I have puppies decorating the calendar. How cute! What activities and ups and downs will they witness, I wonder, during this month in which they have a front row seat for observing my life?

Calendars are one way for us to keep track of time in our lives and in the world.

Watches are another time-tracking tool. Does yours have a second hand? Mine does!

Click, click, click—the line moves gracefully in a circle, never resting for more than a second, never changing tempo. It's reassuring in some ways, the sturdy predictability of a second.

If someone tells me "wait a second" or "this will only take a second," I can always glance at my sturdy friend on my wrist and observe a click and smile. Whoever is talking to me or needs my help has just misused the notion of time. But it's ok. I understand the expression of speech. It sounds more elegant than "wait 97 seconds" or "this will only take 509 seconds."

The breeze outside has quieted now—Aspen tree leaves are shaking and bobbing softly, just barely moving.

Now the leaves have my full attention, and they work with wind to redeliver their message.

I believe the leaves are saying to be playful and joyful with my notions of time; they also help me think differently about education and where it takes place.

"Yes, you can have your second hand on your watch," the leaves say. "You can pay close attention to the seconds and minutes of life. But don't get stuck zooming in there too long. That's the place people become small and afraid and stressed and worried."

I could sense their message wasn't just about my watch or about time. Like all our best teachers, they were challenging me to grasp the deeper, transformative lesson.

"You use student learning outcomes in your classes," the leaves say, "but what about your student learning outcomes of life? All around you is Mother Nature's vast classroom, and she is a generous teacher. And Mother Nature is also very wise, look at how many helpers she has, including us!"

They know me so well, these thoughtful beings. I feel such gratitude for their sharing of lessons I need to learn; their generous teachings are like a beautiful gift I can place inside a basket. These nourishing lessons will sustain me in the seconds, minutes, hours, days, weeks, months, and years to come. Lessons that, if I continue to learn from them, will help me become proficient in the student learning outcomes of life that I believe Mother Nature is hoping I'll grasp. I ponder what I believe would be on her syllabus. I think something like these four learning outcomes would have a place of prominence:

1. Be in respectful relation with place.

2. Honor all of my relatives, human and more than human.

3. Continually demonstrate caring, connection, and love—toward myself and all beings.

4. Conduct myself in ways that affirm I am a good ancestor to future generations.

There surely are more lessons I need to learn, but these are a few of the central ones I address in this book, with the full understanding that it is impossible for me to perfectly demonstrate mastery of such simple—yet profound—lessons. Yet, like perhaps in everything that truly matters, the blessing is in the effort. These are not lessons that one learns once and then is forever done learning. Rather, each lesson is a process of learning and relearning—a continual filling of one's basket. In *Fox Doesn't Wear a Watch*, I extend my work from *The Auntie Way*, and I ask readers to use kindness, fierceness, and creativity in thinking through this question: How do you want to live your life?

To help think through the these important lessons, I engage in the timeless Indigenous tradition of storytelling. Our peoples have wonderful stories that teach and model for us the power and potential of collectives. We learn how to conduct ourselves in our stories. Several Tribal Elders have generously shared our traditional stories, including in the exemplary collection *Anakú Iwachá (The Way It Was)*, published in the early 1970s by the Yakama Nation and led by Tux̱ámshish Dr. Virginia Beavert, a masterful Yakama storyteller from whom I am honored to learn. We are excited about our project with Joana Jansen to publish the second edition of *Anakú Iwachá*, due out in 2021 by the University of Washington Press. Indigenous peoples continue to share many examples of contemporary storytelling as well, including in my book *Huckleberries & Coyotes*.

Back at my home, I gaze again out the window, once more paying attention to my more than human relations and being open to the lessons they may share with me today. I see the leaves are really dancing now. Even rain has picked up—wind, rain, and trees have something important to say to me, I can tell.

"Remember to zoom out and pay attention to the seasons…watch the ups and downs and changes and routines all around you in Mother Nature's classroom. Then you'll better see and understand the ups and downs and changes in your life," they tell me in their songs and dances.

I ponder this message. It's a big message that challenges me to move beyond my limited view of time as the seconds, hours, and days in which I fill my planner's tidy squares. I know I need to shift my understanding of time as a commodity—to move beyond the tyranny of a to-do list. Some lessons take more time or are more complex. Some lessons don't come with a to-do list to memorize or cross off—they are deeper and life changing. Such lessons challenge my notion of learning as something I can do in a hurry, a one and done pursuit. I see how the lessons available to me in Mother Nature's classroom are bigger, more expansive, and more likely to help me achieve the student learning outcomes of life that matter most to me. It is a daunting invitation compared to the relatively easy task of scheduling my week full to the brim with appointments and busywork. I feel mild worry. How will I learn everything I need to learn? How can these important lessons even fit in my basket, when it is filled with the busywork of life?

Early spring rain, wind, and Aspen tree leaves are patient teachers. "Learning isn't about filling a basket once and then you're done," they continue. I see how my student learning outcomes in Mother Nature's classroom will be different—much more about process rather than product. My teachers continue, "Look around you. Notice the seasons and changes happening all throughout nature. Your life has seasons too. You can learn from us about moving gracefully through change and continuing to learn. There is so much you can learn and share about respecting yourself and all your relations."

My good teachers can tell I'm at the limit of my understanding. It seems I'm not able to put the finest of their gifts in my basket...yet. Sometimes learning is challenging: when you have a lesson you're learning and you're still in the midst of really grasping it. My teachers can sense I'm too much in my head, worrying and trying to think too hard. They remind me to be attuned to the deeper wisdom available to me, when I connect with my blessed teachers who surround me in Mother Nature's classroom.

"Live your life with the joy and beauty and wonder of a stand of Aspens dancing magically, leaves singing a hopeful chorus tune. See? Like this," they conclude their message for me today, and the leaves are shimmering with beauty.

This book is about seasons, time, and the ebb and flow of life. Stories focus on the wisdom available to us in Mother Nature's vast classroom, where my people have always done our best learning. Since Time Immemorial our people have followed the seasonal rounds to gather our traditional foods in respectful relation to place. Tiichám (land) is sacred to us, a gift from Tamanwiɫá (Creator).

While the lessons I discuss in this book are rooted in timeless Indigenous teachings about place and relationship, we live in a contemporary world with fast food, digital watches and calendars, shopping centers, and flower shops. And, yes, we even use computers, including the one on which I am typing these stories. In these contemporary spaces, our lessons and teachings do not vanish; they are adapted and renewed. Our people have always adapted and renewed, while holding our most precious teachings, lessons, and commitments close to our hearts.

Our people still follow the seasonal rounds, and today we're likely to ride in a car to a special fishing site or bounce along mountain roads in a pickup truck or SUV to our favorite huckleberry patch. Many of us also purchase or trade for our traditional foods. Maybe we'll buy a gallon of berries from a relative to freeze for later use. Maybe a Pendleton or Eighth Generation blanket or a pair of basketball shoes will be traded for deer meat. In this contemporary world, we continue to uphold our traditional relations, innovating as needed.

While watches and calendars might help the concept of time feel more exact and fixed, the more natural, and perhaps better, way of experiencing time is more fluid and less defined by dates on a calendar grid or by number on a digital clock. Mother Nature's classroom helps teach us this. For example, one might be tempted to ask, "When will the huckleberries be ready to be picked?" to which our Elders will often reply, "They are ready when they are ready." Such a wise reply reminds us that Mother Nature and all our more than human relations have a different notion of time—they refuse to be scheduled by a narrow human-centered vision of time; it is not just another appointment one can write or type into a calendar several months or years in advance.

Such lessons encourage us to grasp what is often shared in Indigenous communities as understanding the difference between being "in time" versus "on time." One can be impeccably "on time" yet upon a punctual arrival might be unprepared or unwilling to learn or help. And one can be perpetually "running late" but once they arrive are ready to listen, learn, and help with a generous heart and a kind word. Being "in time" doesn't require one to be late for appointments, of course, but being "in time" is a phrase that reminds us of a different, perhaps higher set of values that urges us to remember why we are going somewhere in the first place—not to punch a time clock but to be present, just like Huckleberries arrive at just the right time.

Our sacred foods are always "in time," and we are encouraged to follow their example. The deeper lesson is that Mother Nature's time unfolds at a unique and perfect pace. Mother Nature helps us be "in time" if we are humble enough to listen and learn, like when an Elder shares with us a lesson from their youth—when the snowmelt on a sacred mountain creates a certain shape we can see from far away, we then know the Huckleberries are ready. Such precious lessons are often held by Elders, who have many decades of practice being in good relation to place. When Elders warn of drastic changes they've witnessed, we are wise to heed their advice to address climate change; doing so is a way of upholding respectful relationships with all beings. We can learn and grow so much in Mother Nature's classroom, if we are willing to be patient, humble, and good at listening and observing when we are in the presence of our human and more than human relations.

Seasons are helpful for us in tracking time, and seasonal weather is a good reminder of the changes and cycles we witness all around us. Weather can be a fun teacher in Mother Nature's classroom. Thus, beautiful winter snow is featured in some of the stories in this book, fitting as our people's traditional storytelling time is in winter. I also include stories about unexpected weather, experienced through travel to different climates. When we leave a familiar place, there are new possibilities and lessons awaiting us, if we are open to them.

In contemporary times, seasons also bring with them holidays that we may look forward to each year, and these have their certain traditions and treats. I include stories about seasonal holidays important on my reservation (and, of course, those seasonal holiday treats—always a reason to look forward in my calendar!), such as Christmas (cookies), 4th of July (ice cream bars), or Memorial Day (beautiful ribbons my family uses for decorations). I also include stories that happen during particular seasons, such as when leaves change colors in a canyon or when fireworks are lit on a hot summer evening. Stories also feature showy plants and trees who live in my garden, and they are important figures in some of the stories, such as wise Niní (Aspen tree), elegant Magnolia tree, and fun Forsythia.

I used to live in San Diego, a place celebrated for perfect year-round weather. It is true that the weather there is mild, and my family loved visiting, especially when it was freezing cold winter weather back home. Sometimes there's a belief that mild climates have no seasons. I disagree. Even if you live in a place with gentle seasonal changes, or a pavement-heavy urban area, Mother Nature's vast classroom still has much to offer you. Go visit the trees, plants, birds, insects, and animals—they will tell you so much. So will the weather. At times the air is dryer (like when the Santa Ana winds visit the coast of Southern California, sweeping in warm, dry air from the nearby desert); sometimes the weather is more humid, and insects tend to thrive more in those times. When do your favorite trees or plants bloom? When is your favorite fruit in season? These are all ways you can be closer to Mother Nature's notion of time.

In your everyday life, pay attention to time, how you measure time, and when you feel like time is moving at perhaps too quick or too slow a pace. What do your teachers in Mother Nature's classroom have to tell you about these concerns? Ask them. They'll answer. They are wise and generous teachers and want to share with you—they want to be in relation with you.

The stories in this book take place on my Yakama homeland and Indigenous homelands where I've been a guest or visitor, and some of these beautiful places include Kalapuya Ilihi (Willamette Valley), Kootenai / Ktunaxa, Pend d'Oreille / Qíispé and Bitterroot Salish / Sqelix$^w$ homelands / (Flathead Valley), Coast Salish lands and waters, Pahá Sápa (Black Hills), and Aotearoa (New Zealand).

And finally, I cannot leave out beautiful, crafty Fox, after whom I've named this book. In traditional Yakama storytelling, Fox is known as the brother of Spilyáy (Legendary Coyote), who is, of course, a famous teacher and trickster in our stories and in many Indigenous story traditions. I wrote another book, *Huckleberries & Coyotes*, that honors the importance of Spilyáy, and I delight in knowing that this book you are now reading keeps us thinking about the importance of families and the many lessons and inspirations that are available to us if we pay attention to what our relatives are teaching. And by relatives I am referring to both humans and our more than human relations.

One of these special beings who is currently teaching me is Luts'alí (Red Fox). I never know when I'll see Luts'alí, so I keep an eye out in hopeful anticipation. Lessons that Luts'alí teaches me include the need to slow down and be open to the wonder all around me. How else can I even spot this generous teacher if I don't take the time to pay attention and witness? Whenever I see Luts'alí, they are moving elegantly, never looking rushed or stressed. How wise Luts'alí must be to move so gracefully in the world. I have much to learn from this precious teacher. And what a joy it is to learn these powerful lessons in Mother Nature's classroom.

I hope you enjoy this collection of stories and that you connect more deeply and lovingly with the seasons of your own life, with the places and relationships who people your life, and that you soak up the lessons available to you so that you move more easily in your very own perfect pace of life. Seasons differ in all places, and our notions of time differ depending on our inner and outer surroundings; only we can decide what the perfect pace is for us. It is my experience that stories help us to make these important decisions, which ultimately define who we are, and who we want to be, as we move through Mother Nature's classroom.

Each reader brings a unique and important perspective to these stories. Journaling and discussion questions accompany each story so that that as a reader, you may tap into your inner wisdom and reflect more deeply on personal experiences and perspectives, whether reading this book alone or as part of a group. Stories are arranged to help you on your own journey through the book, and, to resist a rigid sense of linear time, they are not ordered by the calendar year. You are, of course, welcome to read the stories in any order you choose.

Thank you for joining me on this journey, as we continually fill our baskets with stories, lessons, and fun. As you move through this book, please take your time. And perhaps most importantly, have a good time!

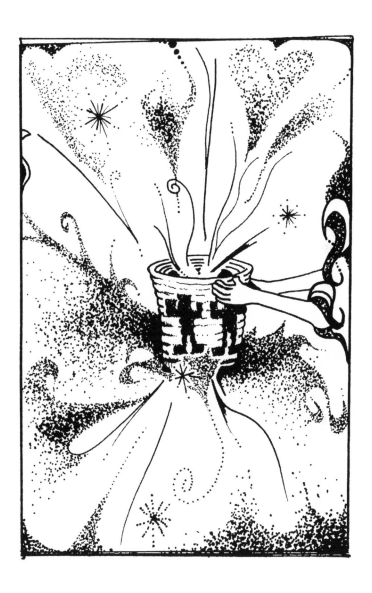

# Springtime Dance Floor

Springtime is a beautiful time. A lot of changes happen on the land. Trees, plants, bushes, birds, insects, animals—they all seem to be eager to step onto the dance floor of growth, renewal, abundance. It's a hopeful, optimistic time.

Sun plays his part, lengthening his workdays. I think he's the conductor for Mother Nature's springtime dance party. Rain and wind join in, taking turns as featured soloists. Wind rustles the trees and leaves with his beautiful tune, spreading pollen, inviting even more beings to the dance floor. I think wind and Aspen tree have a special relationship. How pretty her leaves are, dancing to wind's tune. They shimmer in green and silver beauty.

Rain is another star of the springtime dance party. Clouds work with wind to be in just the right place at the right time. Then rain begins her riff—the strong tapping melody on my metal roof, a delight to the ears of all who hear her. All the plants in my garden, invited or otherwise, soak up rain's beautiful melody. She feeds their souls and gives them strength and encouragement—as all the best music does.

In springtime, there's always one being on the dance floor for whom I keep a special watch. All year long I look forward to her dazzling performance. There's only one in my garden, perhaps fitting because divas usually take the stage by themselves.

This is, of course, Magnolia tree.

I know she's up next on the stage when her warm-up act, Forsythia, is romping on the dance floor. Forsythia—with all the pep and energy of a cheerleading dance troupe, like the kind I saw at the contest at Disneyland one year. The loud music blasting from speakers and all those youth matching the music's beat and energy—perhaps overcoming the energy—with their bouncing, twisting, tapping, stomping, clapping, flying precision.

A display of fierceness and discipline and fun—
Oooooh! Wooooow! The audience exclaims as one
youth flies through the air and does multiple twists.
Aaahhhhh! The crowd says with appreciation as the
flying dancer is caught by peers. The crowd is now
bursting into applause as the dance troupe stomps
and raises their arms in perfect precision with the
last beat of their pop tune music. Their faces shine
with hope and determination. They know this is
their time, and they nailed it, just like Forsythia with
that explosion of bright yellow blooms.

The energy! The intensity!

The first time you see them on springtime's
dance floor, all you can say is, "Wow!"

Forsythia warms up the audience.

And then regal, majestic Magnolia tree
enters the dance floor and says, in a friendly way,
"Step aside, sweetheart," to young Forsythia.

Magnolia can get away with things like this
because she's an Elder. I read she's thought to be
the oldest flowering being on Mother Earth. Wow!
Those millions and millions of years of getting her
showy display just right for her time on spring's
dance floor, it shows. I love her large pink and white

petals. They seem to float all around the branches and trunk. They look delicate but are in fact quite sturdy, strong, fierce, and, of course, beautiful. When she's on the dance floor, I take time each day to admire her performance. She's masterful.

Springtime is such a wonderful time of year, full of hope and optimism. I see all the beings in my garden so eager to grow and share their gifts—to reach their potential. I'm so grateful and inspired. They invite me to the dance floor. What will my contributions be?

Discussion/Journaling Questions for
"Springtime Dance Floor":

1. Name a plant, flower, or tree you enjoy seeing. What characteristics would you say they have?

2. "Springtime Dance Floor" is a story about being inspired to grow and share one's gifts. What gifts do you have that you want to share with the world?

# When Summer Is Winter

Part of the joy and excitement of travel is to see new places and to take a step away from our everyday routines. Sometimes when we travel we are fortunate to experience different weather than we're used to, and it can open us to different ways of learning and understanding. Such is the case with this story.

One sunny summer June morning, I left the U.S. to visit Aotearoa, Māori homeland, New Zealand. When I arrived there, it was winter! Everywhere was gorgeous: the mountains, valleys, and especially the beaches. Surfers know this, as they glide along the beautiful waves. But the most beautiful place I visited was a Māori language nest school

in Hamilton, New Zealand. I observed classrooms
of children as young as infants up through elemen-
tary school. Some children played barefoot on the
dirt and grass outside the school buildings, and
how wonderful it was to see them. Their walk-
ing, running, playing, and being at ease—joyfully
moving across the surface of their Mother, the earth.
Winter here on the North Island is mild compared
to my homeland.

I admired how the school is a community
space, a family space, a space that honors the Indigenous teaching that babies are welcome at our places
of learning. We learn from them and they from us.
Indigenous language is ever present, immersive,
in this precious revitalizing nest. The work in this
sacred language nest resists the settler colonial
vision of schooling that ignores and eradicates Indigenous ways of knowing and being. At the end of my
visit, the entire school was called together outside
to dance and sing us farewell, a parting gift to visi-
tors to fill our ears, eyes, and hearts with good spirit.

The children sang with full, proud, and
confident voices, heads held high and engaged in
a beautiful dance showing us who they and their
ancestors are. It was a model of education in which
the practice of culture shows the children, and any

lucky witnesses, the power of the collective. We carry their blessing with us still. Schools as blessed places—this is a lesson I love thinking about, dreaming about.

The children demonstrated an important example of learning at the right pace. When skills are learned and demonstrated, sure, individually skilled singers or dancers are needed and that's beautiful—to see masterful demonstration. However, it pales in comparison within an entire school of all skill sets and experiences doing their best to work together—the older, more experienced children guiding the younger ones. The inexperienced or new students know their roles are important as well; they are expected to stand with the collective and learn through doing. There is no shame or fear in being earlier on in the learning process. Everyone is acknowledged as an important and necessary part of the collective. It is a shining example of learning and growth at just the right pace. It is a system in which all learners are welcomed and affirmed.

Wow, those children show us, through their strength and determination, anything is possible. Within the beauty of the collective I also see how the current generation feels a deep sense of gratitude to Elders and ancestors and such a hope and respect for the future generations. Looking again at the novices, I see and admire how these children stood amidst their learned peers, aware of their hours and years of practice beyond them. But the newbies are understood to be an important part of the collective. They learn to stand there, rightfully taking their place. They belong. They stand barefoot, connected to Mother Earth, and watch their peers. They take it in; they are a part of the collective learning process that is always unfolding. The novices follow the more experienced children's lead; novice movements are one to two seconds behind, yes, but I do not see it as being out of step.

Rather, they are like the waves on the shore of this Māori island homeland.

I see a ripple effect.

The new students are a part of that same wave as their more experienced classmates, just breaking a bit further behind.

A larger lesson is here. All of us cannot, nor should we all, be at the crest of the wave. If this were the case, the only waves to exist would be the pounding of a strong beach break. If you've ever seen one, you know what I mean: Boom! The long beach break wave rises and falls all at once. It shakes the ground and makes the beach sand steeply angled and hard to walk on.

By contrast, the novice students remind us of the beauty and fun of a long breaking shoulder of a wave. There is room for everyone on this wave of Indigenous self-determination.

We're waiting for you on this wave that will change the world.

What a precious lesson to learn and hold. I'm grateful I got to experience winter in summer and the many gifts this beautiful place and people shared with me. On the plane ride home, journeying in the air above Atáchiish (Pacific Ocean), the big body of water that connects so many Indigenous peoples, I thought of the Ichishkíin motto gifted by Tribal Elders that guides the program I work with at the university, Sápsikw'at xtúwit naamí tanan-mamíyau (Education strengthens our people). What a blessing and inspiration to see these words enacted into truth. Join us. You may have heard: the future is Indigenous.

Note: You can read more about the motto that guides the Sapsik'ʷałá Program here: https://blogs.uoregon.edu/sapsikwala/

Discussion/Journaling Questions for
"When Summer Is Winter":

1. Think of a time when someone younger than you taught you an important lesson. Describe it. How does the lesson continue to have an impact on you?

2. In "When Summer Is Winter," the narrator describes the beauty of a group in various stages of learning. Have you ever been earlier or later in learning something compared to your peers or relatives? How did you feel? How might you feel different if you understood yourself as being on a beautiful wave and that your learning was happening at just the right pace?

# 44 Seasons

The seasons are a symphony of colors and temperatures, soothing and divine, yet so surprising at times. I got to hear the famous symphony The Four Seasons, by Vivaldi, played at a concert hall. I love that music and how it can transport the listener across time, place, and space. You can hear the weather changing through the seasons in the pep or solemnity of the string instruments and their supporters as they work their way through the musical score.

Seasons vary by geography, of course; they're relative. If you've ever been in a really different climate than you're used to, you know how this lesson jumps up and bops you on the nose. I'll tell you about a few examples that I've experienced. I'm from out West, and our summers are typically dry, so imagine my surprise when I got hit on the nose with humidity one time in August in Chicago. I remember putting my running shoes on with grand ideas of how far I'd run alongside the gorgeous shore of Lake Michigan. Uff da! It's bewildering how hard it is to breathe while running in heat and humidity. Back into the conference hotel. Oh no, now I'm chilled to the bone. By the time I got off the elevator, the hotel's AC cranked to the max, my teeth were chattering.

Later, I met a fiercer humidity in July in Louisiana. Wow! I felt I could reach out and ring water out of the air like a dish rag. One fall, I found myself in Havana, Cuba. I remember sitting on the rooftop of the apartment building of the young family we were staying with and how our host rubbed his goose bumped arms, feeling chilly in the 70-degree weather, while we sipped café con leche and watched the cool old American cars cruise the Malecón.

These are all examples of surprising (to me) warm climate, but we can find ourselves in cold that surprises us too. I'm thinking now about the time we decided to drive to Alaska up Highway 97 and onto the famous Alcan Highway in the middle of winter. We hoped to reach Anchorage to see the start of the famous Iditarod, but the driving was much slower than we'd planned. Dry, dry snow causes a white-out each time you meet a car or truck going in either direction. It was on this trip that my body learned the difference between cold, 10 degrees Fahrenheit, and really cold, negative 30 degrees Fahrenheit. I also learned not to leave anything with liquid in the cab of the pickup overnight. That poor orange I left up there one night, frozen solid the next morning, probably the worst way to go for that warm weather fruit.

Well, on that trip, we ran out of time and money and had to turn off the Alcan and head through Carcross Tagish homeland, to Tlingit homeland into Skagway to catch the ferry to Bellingham and the homelands and waters of Coast Salish peoples farther south. What a gorgeous ferry ride. It was winter, you know, so there was a bit of chop on the water at times. Of course, we could not resist taking a bit of fresh air now and then on the deck. We'd hear the water hit the ferry, causing big splashes. It sounded great: Boom! Splash! And then we noticed after the water splashed up alongside the ship and began falling back down, it would turn into snow and ice. Wow! So pretty!

Boom! Splash! Pretty!

Boom! Splash! Pretty!

The air, water, ice, snow, and huge ferry all had their own wintertime waltz going. I felt lucky to see it.

At the end of our trip, when we got back to my reservation, my family heard our assorted tales, the frozen orange, the frequent whiteout driving conditions, the frozen sewage and water system in our truck camper. They shook their heads in amazement or pity.

"Would you do it again?" they asked, always the curious-but-polite question we ask people who've miscalculated something.

"Of course!" we eagerly replied, "As soon as we can!" They smiled and laughed, satisfied their question had allowed our true characters to shine.

It's been several years since I've been to any of these places.

I still feel the same. Can't wait to go back.

I love home. I love where I'm from, with the comfort and familiarity of seasons and place that you know and love as a close relative.

But I also love being surprised by the variations in the seasons. The air, the land, the water, all the trees and other countless beings who share our surroundings—they all change so much if you pay close attention throughout the seasons.

So many changes it can dazzle you. It's magical. It makes me ponder with joy and wonder—if Mother Nature can bring about so many beautiful changes, maybe I can too.

As I think about it, I believe someone mistranscribed Vivaldi's score.

I do believe there are 44 seasons.

Discussion/Journaling Questions for
"44 Seasons":

1. Describe a time when you were in unfamiliar weather. How did it feel to learn something new about seasonal weather?

2. Describe a challenge or failed plan that you nevertheless enjoyed and would be eager to try again. Why do you want to try again? What would you do differently?

# 4th of July on the Rez

On my reservation, the 4th of July is a very big deal.

It seems odd if you think about it. A bunch of brown people spending their hard-earned U.S. dollars on explosives made in China to celebrate a bunch of white guys back East winning a battle against a bunch of other white guys they didn't want to pay taxes to. But like many things, perhaps there is a deeper story. My Nez Perce friend reminds me of the history of Indigenous resistance to settler state oppression that's linked to the 4th of July. As Indigenous dances and gatherings were outlawed as "savage" practices, Indigenous peoples brilliantly began "celebrating" on the 4th of July, and

Indian agents responsible for controlling the Natives assumed such celebrations were motivated by patriotic fervor, evidence that the Natives were appropriately assimilating. Indigenous resistance and resilience is powerful and beautiful.

And yet, for me, 4th of July still, in part, conjures up images of those early colonizing white guys in knickers and powdered wigs celebrating their own ideas of freedom while taking Indigenous lands. I remember hearing the story of how they dressed up as Indians and threw tea in the sea. Strange men. But maybe we're kindred spirits in a way. As Tribal members, part of our sovereign rights include the fact that we don't have to pay state sales tax when purchasing goods on our reservation.

The next time I go through the Dairy Queen drive-through and get a box of Buster Bars I will try to remember to give a little tip of my Mariners baseball cap as I say "No tax" into the drive-through speaker and remember those long dead white guys on the other side of Turtle Island, who'd likely be amazed at the ease of which this sovereign right of mine is exercised and upheld, at least usually. Sometimes I can only sigh in disappointment, as in my experience sometimes the white women who work drive-through can be difficult about the tax-exempt status of Tribal members. They resent it, I think, and so they demand to see the enrollment card, authorized by the Bureau of Indian Affairs in Washington, D.C. You see, it is up to the individual cashier whether or not they will uphold Tribal members' right to be exempt from sales tax on goods purchased on our reservation.

So, one can find oneself sitting in an idling car, holding up the line as the cashier demands the ID card. Once she has it, she takes a long look at it, critiques the photo, looks back and forth between the card and you.

Now we're all kind of gagging on the exhaust from the idling car, sitting here so long while she decides whether to hit the tax-exempt button on the cash register. We all know she only has to type in the enrollment number, take the money, and send us on our way, but there's an interesting kind of power play at work here.

Power, freedom, sovereignty…these are big topics. I'm fascinated with how they play out in our everyday lives; these words, so small and simple on the page, yet really, they mean everything. They are our past, our present, our future.

We learn them in our traditional stories.

We affirm them in our Treaty.

We enact them when we care for our Elders and children.

We uphold them by caring for Mother Earth and ourselves.

Grab your lawn chair. Get comfortable, surrounded by loved ones in a loved place on a hot summer evening. Sure, go ahead. Unwrap a Buster Bar. Watch the kids light fireworks and join in the "Ooooohs" and "Ahhhhhs" of multiple generations, admiring the colorful bursts on display late in the evening, when the summer sun finally sets.

The fireworks are fun and beautiful, but they pale in comparison to the beauty and strength of our people. It might be strange for Indigenous peoples to celebrate on this day honoring the independence of the settler colonial state that has done so much violence to our peoples; yet we are proud to be here, still, on our homelands, in respectful relation to place and in our strong and resilient communities. In that way, we continue to uphold the legacy of Indigenous resistance that at first glance may seem contrary or assimilative. Take a look around—all of this land we now call the U.S. is beautiful Indigenous homeland. I smile in gratitude for the power, freedom, and sovereignty I see all around me, in us.

# Journaling/Discussion Questions for "4th of July on the Rez":

1. What does the 4th of July mean to you? Do you see any contradictions around how it is celebrated in your community, or a community you've observed? Describe the celebrations and their meanings.

2. Describe a time when you or someone you know felt disrespected at a store. What about the interaction felt disrespectful? Which important values were not upheld in the interaction? How do you or your family/friends normally uphold those values?

# Smart as a Log

We are camping for the first time this summer.

I love it.

I feel instantly and exponentially better.

I knew I needed to go to the mountains. I felt it. The tightness of my shoulders, the mild aching in my head, the tightness in my jaw—all signs telling me I'd been working too hard. I'd been overdoing it. I needed to get more in tune with Mother Nature's teachings and pace of life. Recalibrate.

And so, I camp. It's one of my favorite ways to be immersed in Mother Nature's classroom, where I can more clearly focus on my student learning outcomes of life. It is here I am learning:

Slowing down.

Getting away from a screen, an overflowing email inbox, too many hours on Zoom.

Paying more attention to Mother Nature than the problems in my life.

My problems fade and shrink. What takes their place? The smell of the forest, the clear glacier-fed lake, the muted rainbow colors of river rocks—elegant and fun all at once. The rocks smile up at me from the very bottom of the crystal clear lake.

Someone has left freshly cut wood in our campsite. Perhaps remnants of a windstorm tidied up, perhaps big rounds meant for adding to a roaring fire. Perhaps as a left undone to-do task, firewood not yet chopped into handy pieces—you know the kind, the size of the ones out in front of stores, all wrapped up in Saran Wrapped-looking bundles? And, of course, any fire builder knows some nice, dry kindling is needed too.

Nope.

These big rounds here at our site have not

been chopped. They have not been splintered into kindling to start the fire.

They stand or lie at attention, waiting to see what is next.

And this is just fine. Perfect, actually. They just rest. They're curing without needing to do anything at all.

Just cure.

They become my cure.

Their fragrance is beautiful. They cure themselves. Just await the sun, the wind, the still air, the rain, the hail.

How will I cure myself?

Oh! I am. I sit beside these resting pieces of tree trunk, these logs.

I become one of them.

Not really. But I try.

They are my teachers. I hope to be as smart as a log. How lucky I am to sit beside these logs today.

I'm curing.

# Discussion/Journaling Questions for "Smart as a Log":

1. In "Smart as a Log," the narrator describes physical signs of overwork. What are your signs of overwork/burnout? How can you engage Mother Nature's classroom to help cure yourself?

2. In "Smart as a Log," the narrator finds a "left undone to-do task" to be inspiring. What's a current or previous undone to-do task in your life that could be a teaching or blessing to you?

# The Smell of Fall

I love sports. And I love watching loved ones participate in sports. This is one of the great joys of Auntie-ing. Sometimes I'm able to rearrange my work schedule so I can see my niece and nephews participate in sporting contests. Since most of them play so much basketball, my sports viewing usually happens in a gym.

Wapato fans have a reputation for packing the stands and, yes, for being a bit rowdy. Fans being ejected from a game—it's not an everyday occurrence, but I've seen it lots of times. Our fans are typically not shy about telling the refs when they got it wrong. It makes me smile to think about it, those dedicated fans speaking back to authority.

Doing their best to speak up for and protect their loved ones competing out on the floor, whether the athletes are six years old or fifty-five years old. It's not uncommon to see a sweet grandma do her best to stand up on arthritic knees and point her finger at the referee and, in the loudest voice we ever heard from her, give him very pointed, shall we say... constructive criticism.

Our fans seem happiest when our beloved team on the floor is able to enact a version of Rez Ball: fast-paced, with graceful quick passes, the accuracy of *swish*! the ball going effortlessly through the net when a basket is made, whether from inside the key or out beyond the 3-point line. Then a quick transition back into a frenzied, effective defense, forcing another turnover, and:

Pass, sprint, pass, swish!

Yeah!!! We all cheer and clap or whistle loudly in approval and admiration. The noise of our fans fills the gym completely.

Rez Ball can rack up 10 or 12 points with dizzying speed. When this happens, the other team's coach likely calls a time-out, and our fans, all packed together in the stands, give our team another raucous standing ovation. This is, of course, annoying to the other team's fans but…too bad. We all paid our $5 to get into the game and celebrate our loved ones. We will cheer fiercely for them.

So that's typically how a basketball game goes. And it's hands down our community's favorite.

But there are other sports. Some take place outside in Mother Nature's classroom. Some contests happen in an apple orchard on a Saturday afternoon. These contests don't draw so many of our fans. But as you know, I love sports, and Uncle Chris in particular loves watching this sport: cross-country running. When we're able, Uncle Chris and I load up into the car and drive north through Union Gap and along the Yakima River. Keep your eyes peeled for special sightings along our gorgeous river, who sustains life in this place. We are so lucky to be able to see and touch the sacred, anytime we wish.

Oh look! There's K'ámamul (Bald Eagle)! Beautiful!

We eventually head west and up into the hills in the northwest area of the Yakima Valley. It's a bit of a drive from the reservation, but it's pretty out there, the rolling hills and beautiful contrast of leaves beginning to turn—doing their autumn show.

Of course, this is all Yakama Indigenous homeland, and it's good to be in this place, to reconnect and show gratitude to this land now known as ceded territory, taken by the U.S. government in the Treaty-making process in the mid-1800s. Even though the U.S. maps erase our Yakama people's history and relationship with this land, we still honor our relation with place. This land has known our Tribal people for countless generations, Since Time Immemorial, as our Elders say.

Eventually we get to our last turn and then head onto a bumpy, makeshift parking lot adjacent to the apple orchard. We park and then get out of the car and stretch. Ahhhhh! Breathe in that fall time air. Mmmmm…

We walk over to the main spectator area. There are no stands to sit in, and in our rush out the door, we forgot lawn chairs. That's ok. We can stand and spectate. We see the blue, white, and gold uniforms of Wapato and pick out our loved one, sometimes our niece, sometimes our nephew. We make small talk with the few other fans we know. Then the crowd prepares—the young athletes are all lining up for the mass start. And they're off!

We jockey into position so we can yell a word

of encouragement to our loved one. We tell them, "Go!" "Good job!" "Alright!" and perhaps add a "Woohoo!"

And then…all the runners disappear behind a hill.

Cross-country fans know this time—of waiting. The contest is happening, but you can't see it.

We jockey into a new position, on a slight uphill later in the course so we can get a photo and also cheer encouragement.

Soon the athletes are running by again.

"Good job!"

"Use your arms!"

"You can do it!"

"Come on!"

These are common cheers from fans and coaches.

It is an interesting sport, cross-country. Yes, it is about individual effort, yet points of the team's top runners are added up so the winning runner isn't necessarily on the winning team.

I like how individual and collective excellence are intertwined, and the final outcome is kind of mysterious as the competition unfolds.

When our loved one runs by, I snap a photo while Uncle Chris yells. He really gets into it. He's a serious XC fan.

Soon the race is over. We find our loved one and congratulate them on their effort. I show the photo I took on my phone, and they smile. This generation is used to seeing instant digital representations of themselves. I still think it's kind of miraculous. I text or email the photo to family members who were not able to attend the race today.

Then we say goodbye and walk back through the orchard, breathing in the unmistakable harvesttime smell. If you've ever had a ripe apple in your lunchbox and you breathed in that aroma, it's like that, except with millions of apples all surrounding you. Mmmmm...

The smell is strong and hearty, much like the runners we saw today and the fans who trek out into the orchard to encourage them. I believe the runners, with each strike of their feet on the ground, are in a blessed union with Mother Earth. How lucky we are to witness it.

## Discussion/Journaling Questions for "The Smell of Fall":

1. In "The Smell of Fall," the narrator describes fans "speaking back to authority." Think of a time when you or someone you know spoke back to authority. What values were being upheld when you did so? Have you ever been in charge and had someone speak back to you? How did (or would) you handle that?

2. In "The Smell of Fall," the narrator describes liking when "individual and collective excellence are intertwined." Do you feel similarly? Why or why not?

# Springtime Lesson on Kalapuya Ilihi (Willamette Valley)

I feel confused, uprooted, off balance, bewildered.

You see, pain and hurt has enveloped my loved ones recently, plunging us into deep grief.

It's one of those times that the more you fuss over it, the worse it gets.

When a loved one dies, the instinct can be to try and ratchet things down. Squeeze all things around you with tight, tight fists trying to grasp solidly onto something, anything, just to feel like some little bit of life is under control.

Life is a version of fingernails digging into

the palms of your hands with stabbing pain, almost drawing blood. Shoulders, neck, and back aching for no real reason, except for carrying a burden we know we don't have to but somehow can't let go.

Not yet.

Deep down, we know our loved one, gone now to the Spirit World, doesn't want us to be miserable and suffering. Yet the pity and grief surround us like a thick, hazy smog. It chokes us.

It's the feeling of everything and nothing. All at once.

The splintering fog. The screaming silence.

Grief is bewildering. It's impossible to carry alone.

Fortunately, we're not alone.

Tamanwiłá (Creator) has placed helpers and teachers all around us.

When I'm able to remember to stop digging my fingernails into the palms of life, I do something brilliant and wise.

I sit under a tree.

Any tree is good, but I especially enjoy the

company of Papsh (Douglas-fir tree).

My work as a professor and much of my family are based here on Kalapuya Ilihi, the homeland of Kalapuya peoples. And let me tell you, it is a beautiful place.

Two-hundred-feet-tall Douglas-fir trees paint the hills green. More shades of green than your mind can imagine on its own.

Sometimes in a brief and fleeting moment of genius, I sit underneath these wise trees, who have witnessed and survived so much.

In springtime, a breeze often joins us in the early evening.

I sit slouched way down in my chair and rest my head on the chair's back, so I can see way up high and watch the tall tree tops, who stand nearly 20 stories above me.

They sway and move, so gently and gracefully. No lectures. No barking orders or instruction. Just a gentle swaying.

A modeling.

A demonstration.

"See? Like this," I think Papsh may be whispering.

I admire the beauty but fail to learn the lesson, not meeting the student learning objective in my classroom of life.

I spend the night in fitful sleep and wake up feeling miserable, again. Ready to break and shatter under the burden no one's asked me to carry.

I look out the window and see my Uncle-Auntie Teacher Trees. They're waiting patiently, ready to repeat the lesson for me, as needed.

I think back to last night's tutorial, my Uncle-Auntie Teacher Trees swaying gently in the breeze.

"Oh!" I exclaim in a whisper to myself. My eyes flood with tears of recognition and relief, a hard lesson finally coming into focus, like a child struggling to learn to tie a shoelace and finally getting it. That relief of learning, really learning something, and having that awareness to see and understand the exact moment it happened.

I don't have to splinter and break with every challenge. Like my Uncle-Auntie Teacher Trees, I can sway in the breeze. I can be like that gentle and graceful dance of the treetops, strong roots holding me in place.

Just sway. Just sway, like gentle, wise, strong Papsh.

Today, I've met one student learning outcome of life. This hard-earned wisdom-knowledge makes me stronger; I'm able to survive this choking smog of grief. The spring breeze that inspires the gentle swaying of Papsh also clears the air. I can breathe. I can live.

I wipe my tears and gaze back out the window, wondering what my next lesson will be here on beautiful Kalapuya Ilihi.

Discussion/Journaling Questions for "Springtime Lesson on Kalapuya Ilihi":

1. In "Springtime Lesson on Kalapuya Ilihi," the narrator describes trees who are kind and generous teachers. Describe a time when someone was kind or generous to help you through a difficult time. How have you been a kind or generous teacher for others?

2. Describe a time when you failed to learn an important lesson, and you later grasped the lesson. What does this "hard-earned wisdom-knowledge" mean to you?

# Summer Fun in the School Year

Probably like all teachers, I think summer is fun. If we don't arrive at this conclusion on our own, we probably can't help but soak it up from our surroundings. Teachers, but especially students, carry the heavy yoke of the school year, constantly lunging toward summer break. Oh, the fun to be had then.

We see glorious images dancing in our heads of warm weather fun in Mother Nature's classroom: playing in a sprinkler or splashing in a swimming pool on a hot day or eating ice cream cones in the shade, trying to lick and bite all the sugary goodness before it melts into a puddle. Did you ever have some of that melty goodness at the bottom of a cone?

Right before you eat the last bite of your cone, tip it like a drinking glass and savor the sweet liquid. Or maybe you got a dipped cone, that chocolate or butterscotch shell, so tasty yet so messy in the summer heat, best eaten outside, but if you're feeling lucky, you can try eating it in the car. What's one more stain on the seat belt strap?

Or perhaps you prefer meat. The summertime smell of grilled hot dogs and hamburgers or ribs marinated in a special sauce. Careful with that lighter fluid!

All of these festive, joyous imaginings have us enduring the long school year. We count down the days, sometimes literally; the "Days until Summer Break" are posted on large posters in the hallway near the cafeteria in the school building that has fluorescent light glaring overhead.

I pretty much like all countdowns. I'm not sure why. Perhaps it's because I have an impatient nature or perhaps I'm like my dog, always excited to see what will happen next. There's something about the thrill of anticipation or surprise, and waiting for summer is probably the biggest hype I see in terms of anticipating the next season. How all those school children watch the clock and the calendar, putting their minds together, collectively urging time to move faster. How teachers do so too, I think, but usually silently, or maybe they only say so in faculty meetings. Let's be honest—the urging and yearning for summer break has an element of "I can't wait until I don't have to see you every day" and "I'll be free of this place in X days."

I think a bit of the "I can't wait to get out of here" message is why teachers are not usually the ones throwing piles of paper into the air celebrating the last bell of the school year, the first moment of blessed summer.

Year after year, I witnessed this as a student, that incredible yearning for summer, and, of course, the end of summer is back to school time, which has its own hype and anticipation.

But some years, some friends wouldn't come back.

Kicked out of school for "discipline problems," code for a variety of things: substance abuse, vandalism, self-harm, pregnancy, fighting on school grounds, excessive tardiness or absences. I never really understood how if you were late or absent too many times, you were asked not to come back at all.

It sickens me as I think about all of the youth I grew up with who left school and no one bothered to invite them back. We are all poorer for it.

I read the stats and see not much has changed, with students of color and low-income students still being pushed out of schools. In many ways, it's gotten worse in the era of standardized tests determining one's future more powerfully than ever. We are all poorer still for this, except the testing companies who continue to reap fat profits.

Just think what all that money could do, especially for the communities who need it most. And I'm not just talking about the students; I mean everybody, the school district workers, families, the whole community.

I wrote earlier about the fun and joy and imagination of sweet summer; it's a time full of blessed fun in Mother Nature's joyful classroom. I want to take that sweetness like a big dollop of frosting and spread it all across the school year. Maybe I'll put sprinkles on it. I want to see schools full of children who know that who they are, and where they come from, matter.

And that even if one child considers leaving school, fierce collective outrage and so much flexibility and love in the system would make such an outcome actually impossible.

Where school isn't a place we have to go but a place where we love to be, a place that brings out the best in ourselves and fills our heads and our hearts.

And I want to see in our schools that the systems and rules are governed not only by knowledge but by the deeper wisdom of the heart as well.

Some people might say, "This vision is unrealistic. You just can't put summer fun into the blasted school year! There is no time for such fantastic ideas; we have to get down to business, the business of standardized testing!" I can hear the naysaying voice of the status quo. I imagine this voice wearing a three-piece suit and dress shoes that are uncomfortably too tight.

Well, what does that voice know about the future we want? Our future? So, let's ignore that voice. Let's take our time this summer and dream and imagine what we really want. Our schools belong to us. We came from them. We pay for them. Our schools should serve all of our communities.

As I think about my own students all preparing to be teachers, I feel so hopeful.

This generation has the potential to radically transform our schools.

I'll do what I can to help support them in their dreaming.

That ability to imagine, to be creative and fun, these are the skills most needed in our time.

Excuse me, I need to go make a rubric assessing fun and creativity.

Oops, I think I dripped ice cream on it. That's okay. My students are going to expertly smear frosting across it and top it with a generous handful of sprinkles.

Do you hear that?

That's the sound of hope and love, room after room of students and teachers nurturing each other and themselves as they grow in knowledge and wisdom.

When this happens, sure, they'll still love summer, almost as much as the school year.

## Discussion/Journaling Questions for "Summer Fun in the School Year":

1. Think of one example in school that you felt was hopeful or nurturing. Describe it. Why does that experience stand out in your memory?

2. In "Summer Fun in the School Year," the narrator states the "ability to imagine, to be creative and fun" are the skills most needed in our time. Do you agree? Why or why not?

## Season of Social Isolation

It's a strange time right now. Nearly everyone I know is under a strict shelter in place order.

It's the season of social isolation.

Students, colleagues, collaborators, family, and Elders are all isolated, in a collective attempt to keep everyone safe. Even the place I like to get huckleberry pie is closed.

I realize I could make a pie myself, but, you see, there are certain treats in life for which I have high standards. These are things, experiences, happenings so precious to me that I cannot entertain the happy-go-lucky idea of "Let's just try it and see how it turns out." Because, you see, I enjoy baking, but I stick with relatively low-risk baked goods: muffins from a box, chocolate chip cookies, no-bake cookies. Okay, that's not baking, but they are cookies. I'll even do a Key lime pie now and then, but in my recipe, that's a graham cracker crust and, basically, foolproof.

Yes, foolproof. I guess that's the idea I'm looking for. I enjoy making foolproof treats.

I have a hard time taking that approach with Wíwnu (huckleberry). You see, she's not just an ingredient to be used in a pie.

She's sacred.

She's our sister.

As I do for all of our First Foods, I have a love and respect for her that butter, flour, and even Key lime juice from a bottle don't enjoy.

And, you know, sometimes as we get older, we carry the scars and shame of mistakes made when we were younger.

If I'm totally honest, that's part of what's going on too.

Huckleberry pie is perhaps the most treasured, most beloved, most respected baked good in my family's universe. And because it is currently a time of social isolation, one way I can be close to my family is to take a moment and savor memories of our time gathering together.

When I was younger, one time, I decided to bake a huckleberry pie. I found a recipe and followed the instructions. I knew to get the berries out of the freezer where Mom stored our food to last through wintertime. I admired the dark purple skin of the berries that we'd picked up by our sacred mountain last summer. As the pie baked, it smelled great. Mmmmm. There should probably be an air freshener or perfume called huckleberry-pie-baking-in-the-oven scent. I usually bake during winter, and that fresh summer berry smell, along with the cozy heat of the oven, is a delight. And so, at the appointed time, and when the crust looked golden brown, I took the precious offering out of my mom's wall oven and set it on a rack to cool. She had cleared a space for just this purpose, atop her yellow Formica counters. Space was usually at a premium on my mom's counters. Three meals a day, every day, all year long, she cooked and cleaned for the six of us. Mom's kitchen was a busy place with crowded countertops. She cooked and cleaned for eight of us when Grandma and Grandpa joined us, and upwards.

Always plenty of relatives and friends coming over to eat Mom's made-from-scratch, delicious meals.

Leftovers were not real common. We always had so many people crammed around the dining table.

"Clean it up," or "Knock it out," the last person to scrape food out of the pan was told, encouraged to eat the very last of the food. Or if Elders were present, they would eagerly take what they called "care packages" or "doggie bags" home with them, the terminology depending on their humor.

We know no one ever fed Mom's food to their dogs, but this was a time when restaurants, at least in Yakima, called it a "doggie bag" when they sent food home.

So, food and family are rich in meaning and purpose to me and, getting back to my story, there's my very first huckleberry pie, cooling on mom's counter. I'm excited and nervous, full of anticipation.

We have our large family dinner. It's time to cut the pie. The vanilla ice cream has been removed from the freezer and is thawed adequately to make big, round scoops to accompany my masterpiece, which has been carried over to the dining table.

"Michelle, do the honors," someone instructs.

I take the knife, hold my breath, cut into the golden-brown crust.

Something doesn't feel quite right. I keep going, feeling partly confused. I make the second cut and grab the pie spatula, its triangular shape matching the cuts I've just made.

I lift the very first piece of my homemade huckleberry pie.

"Oh, crap," someone says with disgust and disappointment.

My eyes widen. I bite my lip.

"Didn't you thaw and drain the frozen berries before you put them in the crust?" someone asks/barks at me.

I take a breath, putting the sloppy, runny piece of pie into a bowl, doing the best I can to serve my failed masterpiece without splashing huckleberry juice everywhere.

"No, the recipe didn't say to thaw and

drain," I say quietly while keeping on with the serving process. It's kind of pointless to do so, but I don't see a way out.

"That recipe is for fresh berries. You have to do it different for frozen," my education on the spot continues.

"Well, it will still taste good. We can use it like a sundae topping," someone offers with encouragement, trying to bail me out of the deep well of disappointment I've fallen into.

"Can I get a straw to eat your huckleberry pie, I mean, to drink your huckleberry pie?" someone teases.

I feel my cheeks burn with shame, perhaps matching the color of the juicy Wíwnu mess in my mom's Pyrex pie pan.

Somehow, we got through the bad dessert service of that meal.

And guess what? I've never made a huckleberry pie since. I leave that to the pros.

I am grateful to them and admire their skill, including my now sister-in-law; she's a pro pie-maker. Huge respect—I know it's not a foolproof dessert.

It's been at least three decades since my runny pie fiasco. I've made plenty of mistakes, larger and smaller, since then.

Sometimes when we make mistakes, we want to hide away, perhaps out of fear or shame or disappointment. Perhaps we wish for a shelter in place order and strict social distancing, now that we have the vocabulary for it.

During this time today of real social isolation, with the bigger fears and losses of a pandemic, and even minor inconveniences like my favorite pie place being closed, I know that someday, when we are allowed to gather again, my large family will always welcome my efforts to attempt anything that's not foolproof.

I am thankful that beneath the sometimes-crusty exterior, my family has a spirit of love and kindness and generosity that overshadows the teasing and criticisms that we must all give and receive in families.

We will see.

Maybe during one of these cold winter days I will take on the task of baking another huckleberry pie.

If I do, I will be sure to thaw and drain the frozen berries.

And I will bring some straws just in case.

## Discussion/Journaling Questions for "Season of Social Isolation":

1. In "Season of Social Isolation," the narrator describes teasing and criticism that take place in families. Do you ever tease or criticize your family members or friends? How do you make sure they know your love for them is greater than the teasing or criticism?

2. "Season of Social Isolation" is a story about learning from a mistake. What is a mistake you've learned from? How did the difficulty of the task help you admire those who have greater skill?

# Early Spring

Early spring is a fun and dramatic time. You never know what the weather is going to be. One day, it's 65 degrees Fahrenheit and sunny. Get the lawn chairs out; grab my sun hat. We can hardly believe how warm the sun feels on our bare arms after the long winter of being bundled up. I sit comfortably, leaning back in the chair, and feel the warmth of the sun on my face.

The next day, it's 35 degrees Fahrenheit and a few snowflakes. Brrrrr...get my down coat, hat, and gloves back on to walk the dog. A few weeks ago, I would have considered this a warm day; how quickly I've gotten used to the sunny, warm temperatures of late. Such is my experience in Mother Nature's classroom in early spring and every time we are transitioning between seasons. She keeps changing the weather conditions, keeping me alert and observant. I never know what to expect, and I find that to be fun.

My dog is also entertained by these ups and downs of seasonal changes. One moment, he's shedding like crazy in accordance with the warmer temperatures. Those puffs of his hair gathering in clusters on the floor like conference attendees in the lobby just before doors open for a much-anticipated keynote speaker.

Then, when the temperature drops 30 degrees, he's back to growing multiple layers of his thick, pretty fur coat. All throughout this seasonal transition, the cycle will continue. My dog and I both shedding and adding layers as Mother Nature dictates. This must be one of her favorite times of year. She keeps us guessing on what kind of weather we'll experience in her classroom, and we equip ourselves according to her vision. We never question her—in this case, it really is true: teacher knows best.

Sometimes I hear people complain about this time of year, early spring in northern climates. Gardeners are antsy to plant their masterpieces; they see spring begins on a specific calendar date, but Mother Nature reminds us to be flexible. Orchardists on my reservation walk the tightrope of deciding how cold it can be before the frost kills the tree buds and their crops of apricots, peaches, nectarines, and even apples. Although apples are sturdier and can withstand lower temperatures, even these brethren fruits have their limits, and when that happens, the wind machines howl in the middle of the night, moving vast quantities of air so the buds don't freeze. The machines shake my grandpa's old mobile home, where my dog and I awake with a start when the clamor begins.

We both stir with anxiousness at the noise, the shaking. Do you know the feeling, when you know you'll be fine but, in the moment, you still feel afraid? Eventually, the howling machines stop. The sun has come to warm the air, the earth, and our spirits. We hear our teacher, Mother Nature, calling to us, "Come outside and see what you'll learn today!"

That's our cue. Let's bundle up and go for a walk.

Mother Nature welcomes us back into her vast and generous classroom. Once again we are filling our baskets with precious lessons to view each day as a gift and to be open to the new possibilities that change always brings. We've been working on these particular student learning outcomes of life for many years now. We never get bored in Mother Nature's classroom. We are pleased to be part of it. Today when she takes roll, I'll eagerly answer I'm "present"! My dog's face is smiling, and I can see his breath in the chilly air. He's present too.

# Discussion/Journaling Questions for "Early Spring":

1. In "Early Spring," the narrator writes about gardeners antsy to plant their gardens. Have you ever felt impatient for a season to change? Describe how you felt and why.

2. In "Early Spring," the narrator describes knowing that all will be ok but still being afraid or anxious in the moment. When have you felt this way? How did you get through it? Take a moment and honor your resilience.

# Beautiful Pahá Sápa (Black Hills)

One summer day, we visited my Lakota friend and mentor in Rapid City, South Dakota. At our request, he gave us a tour of his workplace and shared about his work to help heal our people and all of society. That's how Indigenous visions of healing work, you see. Yes, we want the one illness in one person/patient healed, and we see how all illness shows us that greater forces are out of balance. To want to heal and help takes great patience. My friend has this.

We walk to a restaurant for lunch. It is a sunny day. Out there on the Plains, the sky is vast. It feels universal. With that wide, wide sky, sun takes the opportunity to really shine. That bright light in the blue sky, such a source of warmth and life.

Seated in the restaurant, our friend encourages us to "Try the buffalo. It's excellent."

Over lunch, our friend tells us many of his favorite places he thinks we should go see and enjoy. The pride and love he has for his people's beautiful homeland shines, like that bright sun outside. Of course, Lakota homeland is endlessly beautiful, so we struggle to remember all of the many places he suggests to visit. Our trip ends before we can see them all. So, we return in the fall. Let me tell you about one of the special places we were privileged to visit.

Fall time in Pahá Sápa (Black Hills) is a gorgeous time of year. We took our friend's suggestion to drive up to the hills and through Spearfish Canyon. Wow! Those granite walls and all the trees! Masses of trees! Some tall pines, who stand tall and strong, their green serving as a gorgeous contrast for the brownish land, and the stars of the canyon at this time of year: the endless fluttering of yellow, golden, buttery colored Aspen tree leaves. The leaves dancing in the mild breeze—their delicate movement looks a bit like an army of butterfly wings—such graceful beauty.

"Wow!" we say.

We try to capture the gorgeous scene with our cameras, but it is impossible. Such beauty cannot be contained in one frame.

We take our time, ooooohhhing and aaaaah-hhing around each twist and bend of the canyon road.

We finish our journey through the canyon and visit other special places, including the Buffa-los in Custer State Park. If you ever get a chance, I encourage you to go visit that sacred land with a horrible English name; witnessing the large, wise Buffalos is worth it. Yakama peoples have a tradi-tional story of why we don't have this blessed rela-tive in plentiful numbers on our homeland. In brief, the story shares that due to Coyote's lack of patience and respect toward women, our homelands would not be blessed with large buffalo herds. It is a story that teaches us of the sacredness of women and the importance of honesty, respect, patience, and trust. From a respectful distance, I look into one Buffalo's eye and greet them in my language. I believe they understand, as Buffalos know my land and language from Legendary times.

These hills who've seen so much violence,

theft, and greed over the years. Settler colonialism, broken treaties, lust for profits from extraction—these all have scarred the land.

Yet it remains a sacred place, those bold granite walls and peaks and masses of trees who model renewal for us as they grow and lose their leaves every year.

There's a strength and resilience in the land and among the people.

Look up and see the highest point, Black Elk Peak.

Note: You can learn more about the Black Hills Center for American Indian Health at https://www.bhcaih.org

# Discussion/Journaling Questions for "Beautiful Pahá Sápa":

1. In "Beautiful Pahá Sápa," the narrator describes a generous and patient mentor. Who is someone you've known who shares these gifts? Write a note to thank them. If possible, send it.

2. Name a place where the beauty was impossible to capture with a camera. Who are the people Indigenous to that place? Take a moment to learn more about the people whose homeland you admire.

# Memorial Day Fashion Show

I remember the pink construction paper I used one spring to make the cover of my first book. I believe I was six years old. My book was duct taped together, and I admired the soft pink pages meeting the shiny gray tape that held together the contents of my first real written story. The color of the paper is vivid in my memory—the same color as the pink carnation crayon in the big box Mom bought for me at the beginning of the school year.

And the crayon color's name was true; I saw real pink carnations at the Wapato Flower Shop when I went there with Auntie. She was shopping for florist ribbon, she told the attendant. I didn't know that was the name of the ribbon we stored in shoeboxes and that I tied around the headstones at our family members' graves in the old Indian cemetery on our reservation.

We have lots of dead people. They are part of our family. They are our loved ones, even if we never knew them personally—they are still important to us, and we remember them in stories and prayers. They watch over us and help us.

Part of our tradition includes sprucing up their graves at least once a year, always around Memorial Day. It might be kind of strange, but I really enjoy cemeteries. I love the quiet peacefulness and witnessing the neat rows of monuments, whether grand or humble, to people who have lived their lives here on Mother Earth, whether for a long or brief time, and now are in the Spirit World. In cemeteries, we are surrounded by Mother Nature—with dark green grass or soft brown dirt under our feet and the wide, wide sky above us. On clear days, we can look West and see Pátu, our beloved Mount Adams, who has always loved and cared for our people.

When I was younger, I used to think of our cleaning and tending our loved ones' graves as a kind of fashion show. My job was to get our dead people all decorated with beautiful colors of ribbons. I usually went along with heteronormative expectations in the color scheme: pinks and purples for women, reds and browns for men.

But some graves had their names worn off the tombstones, the work of sun, wind, dust, rain, snow, ice, and hail over the many, many years. So, on these people, I'd just guess, use my intuition when I reached into the Nike shoebox to grab the spool of florist ribbon I'd provide for my relative who died before I was born.

And sometimes I'd engage in some playful gender bending. Maybe Great-Grandpa would get ribbon that was more pinkish than red. I remember feeling creative grabbing the spool that had "Dragon Fruit" stamped on its cardboard exterior and decorating Great-Grandpa with it; I smiled a little to myself. I was at the age of youth in which intuition was still trusted. No one questioned me on it and besides, he had all those gorgeous, feminine pink peonies standing at attention atop his grave; all the many flowers tucked neatly into their vessels—old jam jars whose labels were neatly removed, emptied and cleaned Yuban coffee containers from my fancy California Auntie, and empty MJB coffee cans from my thriftier Grandpa who lived on our reservation.

All year long we saved up containers that could serve as vases with which we decorated our loved ones. It is a collective effort, and everyone has an important role in helping make sure our loved ones look their finest for the Memorial Day fashion show.

Discussion/Journaling Questions for "Memorial Day Fashion Show":

1. Have you been to a gravesite of a loved one or ancestor? How do you decorate their grave? Or how would you if you got the chance to do so?

2. In "Memorial Day Fashion Show," the narrator discusses learning about gender norms and play-fully resisting them. What gender norms have you learned? How do you resist or uphold them?

## Four Generations

I love winter. The short days that make you prioritize what needs to happen in daylight. Wintertime can become a busy time with lots of to-dos on one's list, but to me it is always satisfying to take the time to slow down and savor the beauty of winter.

How my steaming hot cup of coffee tastes extra delicious in the calm quiet of predawn. I watch for K'ámamul (Bald Eagle) in a nearby tree.

The excitement of Aan (Sun) finally rising from his slumber and climbing above the mountains to the east. When I see the first light of day, I think I hear him yawning. I think Aan's yawn turns the sky a pink-orange color.

How the snow sparkles like diamonds in the daylight—a carpet of jewels! No wonder my dog delights in romping through the snow—he's canine royalty making first tracks in that pristine powder.

The crisp air that chills my face, my cheeks cold to the touch, like the drinking glasses Auntie kept in the freezer. I remember her pouring orange juice for me and how that frosted glass seemed elegant and luxurious and made me feel special. I'd savor my juice, watching the icy crust form in a ring inside the glass, like when the edges of a lake first freeze in late fall. How the tips of my fingers and thumb would serve as oval-shaped defrosters on the outside of the glass as I held it and sipped, enjoying the contrast of the frozen glass and the juice of the fruit from warm climate.

I remember delighting in the frozen "ponds" that formed in big dips or potholes on our gravel driveway on our reservation and how I'd skate across them, feeling glamorous like the ice skaters I saw in the Olympics on TV. I could imagine myself wearing a pretty sequined outfit skating to beautiful classical music, although I knew the sweatpants and moon boots I wore were actually more comfortable and appropriate for my ice rink only a few feet wide. Still, when I'm done, I think I hear applause and perhaps teddy bears being tossed my way.

To me, winter is a magical mysterious time. A time when storytelling and imagination bring us closer to ourselves and one another.

And when the Creator takes his sugar shaker full of snow and covers our landscape, everything looks peaceful and sacred, kind of like those Christmas village displays I admire at the store, except better.

Those tiny villages show us a kind of beauty, order, and fun. But I think they're missing something. I don't see in them the messy beautifulness of life:

The potholed driveway ice rink.

The splatters on Mom's stovetop from frying up Spam for a hearty breakfast with all the family crowded around the table and enjoying one another's company and the cozy warmth of the fire roaring in the old wooden stove. If your back is sore, take a seat right in front of the stove. It heals you, almost instantly.

I also love the beautiful messiness of flour dust and smudges on the kitchen countertops and cabinets from making butter cookies with my niece.

We use my grandmother's electric cookie press (named the Super Shooter), and with joy we select the first disc that will determine the shape of our sweet and buttery delights. Let's make trees! Now snowflakes! Now Scottie dogs!

Bzzzzz. Bzzzzz. Bzzzzz. The Super Shooter presses dough through the disc, and we see our cute dough creations appear like magic.

Grandma was very thrifty, and poor, and the Super Shooter purchase would have been a big deal to her. I can imagine her standing in the aisle at the Bi-Mart in downtown Yakima hemming and hawing over whether to buy it, her cart and lingering presence in front of the small appliances likely annoying the other customers who had to squeeze around her in those too-tight aisles.

"Waste not, want not" was a saying held close to Grandma's heart, as well as to many of her generation.

That the Super Shooter has now been used by four generations would warm her sensible heart, affirming indeed that the purchase was not in waste.

I imagine Grandma now, in the Spirit World, giving the Creator her firm, determined stare, suggesting to him that he grace us with another generous dusting of snow.

Áw ipúuysha ámchnik! (It's snowing outside!)

Let's finish these cookies and go make snow angels! Then we'll come in, warm ourselves by the fire, and enjoy some of these delicious cookies.

Discussion/Journaling Questions for
"Four Generations":

1. Think of a food or activity you enjoy that connects your family, or friends, of different generations or ages. Who was one of your teachers? Describe a special moment of your learning or sharing that special food or activity.

2. What is a wintertime activity you enjoy? Whether it takes place outside or inside, describe it. How does taking part in that activity make you feel?

# The Circle of Life

Luts'alí (Red Fox) trotted across the backyard today.

We were busy with odds and ends of our morning routine: check my email, wash dishes from last night, prepare breakfast. Sometimes our lives seem full of routines and schedules; like our lives are just a series of watching the clock in between tasks.

We wouldn't have known about Luts'alí if it weren't for our fierce rez dog watchdog who's spoiled and adored almost to a fault (ours, not his, of course). Yet despite our pampering of this dog no one else wanted, he remains true to his duty: to watch over us and growl with suspicion and warning when he sees something out of his preferred and expected order.

That's how it was this fine and chilly early spring morning. We were busy with the busywork of life and GRRRRR!

We heard the loud warning, the deep growl of our dog, meaning he meant business. His communication was effective, as we immediately stopped our busywork and looked out into the backyard, wondering who the offender was.

There was Luts'alí (Red Fox).

Expecting a cat, I was surprised. "Is that a fox?"

"Yes," Uncle Chris confirmed.

"Wow! Look at that pretty bushy tail!"

Just as in the photos and artwork you see: pretty orangish coat, dark feet, pointy snout and ears, a look of cunning in the eyes, and a big showpiece bushy tail.

"Wow! So pretty!"

We watched Fox trot, calmly but with determination, crossing the backyard.

"Is there something in Fox's mouth?" Uncle Chris asked.

"I think so," I responded. Yet Fox was just far enough away I couldn't tell the nature of the cargo.

And then, Fox was gone. Lost to sight in trees, hills, snow mounds taking their time to melt away.

"I'm so glad you told us. Good boy!" I told our dog and patted his head and rubbed his velvety soft floppy ears.

The highlight of the morning was all due to our dog's alertness and ready willingness to share with us what he sees and thinks.

I paused and pondered the larger lesson my dog was teaching me:

How so many of life's highlights are brought to our awareness when we listen to one another, when we really share with one another. When we take a break, even for just a moment, from the busy-work of life.

A moment later, we saw a large cat looking half helpless, half upset, like they had a half- or quarter-hearted desire to try and hunt down Fox.

"Oh!" Uncle Chris and I both said aloud as we had the same thought.

"I wonder if Fox took a kitten."

Hmmmmm…we could imagine Fox snatching up a helpless baby cat for a morning meal.

The circle of life indeed, just like they sang in The Lion King. We saw the famous musical in Las Vegas a long time ago; the beauty and drama of the costumes stay with me; they've carved out their own little place in my memories, and I'm grateful. I'm inspired when I think of the magic of the fabrics' colors and movements imitating nature in a showy and glamorous way. I loved it. Humans using art and drama to tell the stories of dynamic relationships we see all around us in nature, if we really pay attention.

Whether we buy a ticket to sit inside a theater or simply look out the window of our home, the possibilities for inspiration and wonder are endless if we really listen and share. This requires pausing, even for a moment, from the busywork of life. I sometimes need to turn away from the clock, quit fussing over minutes as I look at my watch, and be open and ready to learn, to be inspired. We too are part of the circle of life. How do you want to participate in the drama of life today?

Oh, I forgot to tell you, Fox doesn't wear a watch. Maybe our clever more than human relation is modeling for us a most important student learning outcome of life—take the time to be present in the present. Gosh, that can be a challenge, but I'll try, Luts'alí, I'll try. Come visit and remind me again, Luts'alí, when I forget this lesson! I'll try to keep a watchful eye out, and I know my good dog will too.

Discussion/Journaling Questions for
"The Circle of Life":

1. Describe a time when you really listened or shared with someone. Why did you do so? How did you feel?

2. "The Circle of Life" is a story about learning to shift away from life being "a series of watching the clock in between tasks." Do you ever feel like life is that way? Who helps you shift away from that?

# Conclusion: Generous Teachers All around Us

This morning I saw something really pretty.

I was surprised what an impression the beautiful simplicity made on me.

One of those images out of the millions in our lives that somehow jumps out at you and says, "Hey, pay attention. I'm showing you something."

I love it when this happens, when Mother Nature and her helpers work together to develop and deliver a curriculum tailor made for me. They know at just which level and depth my head, heart, and spirit need a lesson, so that I may grow and learn as a person with increased inner richness and greater appreciation and understanding for the world external to me.

I believe this is education at its finest. It's built to help the individual student grow and succeed, so that each student may confidently and humbly make their contribution to strengthen our collective.

When this kind of education happens in our human-made institutions, it dazzles us.

"Wow! That class was fun!" we might say, the joy and surprise indicating that such an experience is the exception, not the norm.

But in Mother Nature's classroom, we can find a joyous, wondrous lesson every single day if we look for it. She's such a generous teacher. Sometimes she can even sneak a powerful lesson into our lives and minds when we least expect it.

Such is the case for me today.

Well, what did I see? The image, the lesson?

I'll tell you.

I looked out the window resting my eyes, as I periodically do, from reading a book. And there I saw a gorgeous image, Niní (Aspen tree) in early spring.

Now, if you know about Aspen trees, you'll know in early spring they look kind of dead, branches and trunk all white and gray and black. No leaves to be found, no buds, no indicators of life.

So, the tree itself, in this time when plants and trees and flowers are starting to really show their dazzling growth, well, let's just say this big whitish, grayish, blackish Aspen tree is not much to look at.

But then I tilted my head back to rest my head on the back of my grandpa's old rocking chair, my reading chair, and there it was, the image sticking with me:

The tall, tall branches atop the huge Aspen tree are bone white against the robin's-egg blue sky. The branches are so crisply white, they almost look like stripes painted on a blue canvas. The color contrast is stark and beautiful. How impressive to see this tree majestically reaching up to touch the sky.

Wow.

I now have a greater appreciation for Niní, who rests through the winter and waits patiently through the spring before growing their showy leaves. When a slight summer breeze arrives, all those thousands of leaves dance, shimmer, and softly whisper.

Gorgeous.

I share this story to conclude this book because I want to remind us of the power and beauty of the lessons all around us.

Anytime we look or go outside into Mother Nature's vast classroom, we can see, listen, learn, and understand lessons on constant display for us if we have the grace to engage them. Yes, we will still use our watches and planners and digital calendars in these contemporary times. Yet we are also called to connect to other ways of measuring time, in which we connect with deeper lessons available to us from our more than human relations, to witness the seasons, the weather, and all beings with whom we share our environment. We are all invited to continually fill our baskets with the generous lessons available to us in Mother Nature's classroom. What student learning outcome of life will you focus on today?

Even if you live somewhere with gentle seasonal changes and mild climate, Mother Nature still provides a wonderous classroom for learning: plants, animals, insects, birds, weather—they all shift and change and will speak to us...if we listen. Such teachers are helpful and generous as we navigate the busyness in our lives, tracking time with watches and calendars. These ancient teachers can also help us learn about the inner seasons of our lives, as we grapple with changes in relationships and emotions, as we make large and small decisions about how we want to live our lives.

As we near the end of this book, I want to wish you a wonderful day and a life as beautiful and majestic as the tip-tops of tall Niní reaching up and touching the regally blue sky. I wish you a life filled with the fun and playfulness of a thousand Aspen tree leaves dancing in a warm summer breeze.

Oh, look! Fox just sauntered by, and you know what? Luts'alí is not wearing a watch.

# About the Illustrator

Crystal L. Buck is a Native American artist and resides in Spokane, Washington. She is an enrolled member of the Yakama Nation and grew up on the Yakama Indian Reservation. Her passion for drawing and painting evolved at a very young age. She gives credit to her amazing art teachers. They encouraged her and believed in her talent enough to enter her work in local shows throughout the years. Before completing high school, she participated in her first painting showcase where she met and networked with various artists. She sold her first piece in 1997. Upon graduating from college as an Exercise Specialist in 2003, she also received a minor in art with a specialization in painting from Fort Lewis College in Durango, Colorado. Most recently, she collaborated with the Burke Museum in Seattle, Washington, to create signage for their re-opening after COVID-19. Her drawing was selected for the 2019–2020 Washington State Indian Education Program logo. In 2020, Crystal illustrated the books The Auntie Way: Stories Celebrating Kindness, Fierceness, and Creativity and Huckleberries & Coyotes: Lessons from Our More than Human Relations.

Crystal is the mother of four beautiful children and loves spending time with her family. She enjoys participating in traditional gatherings and learning the Salish language with her kids. She's passionate about running, leading fitness dance classes, drawing, and crafting. She is inspired by artistic creations that focus on her Native roots, modern art techniques, Zentangle, vibrant and various uses of colors, lines, and patterns. One of her artistic dreams is to blend her love for hummingbirds and her individual style into a unique thematic masterpiece. You may contact Crystal by email: cry5tal_lea@yahoo.com

# About the Author

Dr. Michelle M. Jacob is an enrolled member of the Yakama Nation and has over 20 years of teaching experience, most currently at the University of Oregon where she is Professor of Indigenous Studies in the Department of Education Studies and serves as Affiliated Faculty in the Department of Indigenous, Race, and Ethnic Studies and Affiliated Faculty in the Environmental Studies Program. Michelle engages in scholarly and activist work that seeks to understand and work toward a holistic sense of health and well-being within Indigenous communities and among allies who wish to engage decolonization. Michelle loves to write and has published six books, including *Huckleberries &*

*Coyotes*, *The Auntie Way*, and *Yakama Rising*. She has also published numerous articles in social science, education, and health science research journals and has been awarded grants from the U.S. Department of Education, the National Endowment for the Humanities, Spencer Foundation, and the National Science Foundation. Her research areas of interest include Indigenous methodologies, spirituality, health, education, Native feminisms, and decolonization. Michelle founded Anahuy Mentoring, LLC, to support her vision of sharing Indigenous methodologies with a broad audience. Michelle is grateful to all her family and friends for their love and support and, of course, keeps learning and re-learning lessons from her human and more than human relations as she continually fills her basket! Unlike Fox, Michelle usually wears a watch and sometimes she even manages to be "in time."

You may contact Michelle through the form on her website, where you can also sign up for her email list to be the first to receive all the news related to Anahuy Mentoring: https://anahuymentoring.com Michelle's blog is https://auntieway.com Michelle is on Twitter: @AnahuyMentoring

# Author Acknowledgments

I am grateful to the fantastic scholars and educators who peer-reviewed this book manuscript: Clint Carroll, Beth Piatote, CC Wright, Lori Tapahonso, and Brook Colley. Chris Andersen, Theresa Jacob, Angie Morrill, and Leilani Sabzalian also offered valuable feedback on the manuscript. Thanks to Alja Kooistra for skillful copyediting. All feedback I received greatly strengthened this manuscript, and any weaknesses remain my own. I am grateful *Fox Doesn't Wear a Watch* is blessed with the beautiful artwork of Crystal Buck.

I've been fortunate to work with many supportive people who have educated me and shown me what it means to be a powerful role model in one's work. Special thanks to my dear colleagues in the University of Oregon Sapsik'ʷałá (Teacher) Education Program, Education Studies, Native American Studies, and Native Strategies. Thanks to the COE Finance team for their kindness and efficiency. Thank you to the wonderful writers and artists at Flathead Valley Community College, the WriteSpeak Program, and the Joy Collective, for encouraging my creativity and growth.

I am so grateful to each attendee of my The Auntie Way Writing Retreats and Professional Development Courses--it is a gift to work with each of you in bringing the teachings of *The Auntie Way* more deeply into our lives and work. I look forward to many more fun and productive gatherings with you!

As with *Huckleberries & Coyotes*, at the time of this writing, it is not safe for Elders to gather with groups to tell stories due to the pandemic we are all facing. Our people have always adapted our traditions for contemporary times, and I hope this book serves as a helpful resource for all peoples who wish to engage stories to learn and grow. In preparing this book, I continued to be inspired by the work I did with Virginia Beavert, Joana Jansen, and Deward Walker for the new edition of *Anakú*

142

*Iwachá,* a tremendously important book of Yakama legends and stories that is scheduled to be published in 2021 by the University of Washington Press.

Hugest of thanks to my family who have given me so much love over the years: Dad, Mom, Uncle Jim, Roger, Gina, Garret, Hunter, Faith, Justin, Alicia, Quintic, Hazen, Blaise, Sealy, and my in-laws, who are a blessing!

I'll end by thanking the world's greatest camping and hiking buddies, Chris and Anahuy. Áwna!

## About Anahuy Mentoring

Anahuy Mentoring is committed to engaging Indigenous methodologies to teach about the importance of Indigenous ways of knowing and being. *Fox Doesn't Wear a Watch* is published by Anahuy Mentoring, an independent Indigenous press that utilizes Indigenous cultural values in peer review.

Learn more and join my email list at https://anahuymentoring.com

Michelle blogs at https://auntieway.com

Twitter: @AnahuyMentoring

Anahuy is the Yakama Ichishkíin word for black bear.

## ANAHUY MENTORING, LLC

EXCELLENCE IN INDIGENOUS METHODS

Also available from Anahuy Mentoring:
*The Auntie Way*
*The Auntie Way* celebrates the love and lessons we learn from our favorite aunts, whether related or chosen, and is available in paperback and e-book from Amazon or your favorite bookstore. You may purchase author autographed copies of *The Auntie Way* at https://anahuymentoring.com
Aunties are awesome!

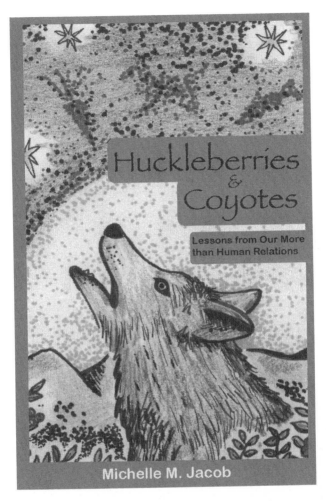

Also available from Anahuy Mentoring:
*Huckleberries & Coyotes*
*Huckleberries & Coyotes* builds upon Dr. Michelle M. Jacob's previous studies of cultural revital-ization and the power of Indigenous teachings by reflecting on what huckleberries, coyotes, and our more than human relations can teach us. This book will inspire you and warm your heart!

# Ready to Learn More?

## Coaching

If you enjoy the approach Michelle uses in her books, perhaps you'd like to spend focused time being coached by Michelle to address the obstacles currently keeping you from reaching your dreams. In this process you will **grow and thrive** in your own kindness, fierceness, creativity, and productivity.

As a coaching clients, you receive 1:1 coaching with Dr. Michelle M. Jacob, renowned Yakama scholar and speaker. Michelle draws from cultural teachings and a wealth of knowledge of the academy to lead you through a **fun** process of creating and using a vision to guide your work, planning, and problem solving. The result is **tremendous growth** in productivity and happiness. Coaching clients have private and confidential coaching sessions with Michelle, as well as access to all Anahuy Mentoring workshops and courses, including the popular The Auntie Way Writing Retreats.

If you're ready for awesome and unprecedented growth, fill out the form on Michelle's Coaching page to learn more.

https://anahuymentoring.com/coaching/

## Support for Your Writing

Join the fun and productive The Auntie Way Writing Retreats, offered throughout the year. In this dynamic group setting, writers of all backgrounds thrive in moving their projects forward. To learn about the next The Auntie Way Writing Retreat, please visit

https://anahuymentoring.com/products-and-services/

If you'd like to book a writing retreat for your group or organization, please contact Michelle at anahuymentoring@gmail.com

## Professional Development Courses and Workshops

Dr. Michelle M. Jacob offers a range of Professional Development Courses and Workshops, including Indigenous Time Management, Having Better Meetings, Meaningful Institutional Service, Making a Writing Plan for Success, Professional Trajectory Planning, and Creative Writing for Joy and Learning.

To learn more please visit

https://anahuymentoring.com/products-and-services/

To book a course or workshop for your organization, please contact Michelle at anahuymentoring@gmail.com

Made in the USA
Middletown, DE
02 November 2022

13973263R00094